GW00492616

Springs of Joy

Augustine
Shakespeare
Goethe
Mozart
Newman

SEARCH PRESS LTD, ENGLAND

KAMPMANN & COMPANY INC, NEW YORK

COPYRIGHT BY LEOBUCHHANDLUNG, CH-ST. GALLEN

Man's heart strives
after unending
eternal happiness.
Thou hast created us,
O Lord, for Thyself
and our heart is
restless until it
rests in Thee.

ST·AUGUSTINE

O lead my spirit,
O raise it from
these heavy depths,
transported by Thy Art
that fearlessly and
joyfully it soar up
to Thee. For Thou,
Thou knowest all
things, Thou alone
canst inspire.

BEETHOVEN

Only one thing is important,
whether we are brave or
cowardly: to be always there
where God will have us,
and for the rest to
trust Him.
There is no other remedy against
fear but to abandon ourselves to
His Will.

BERNANOS
✝

Only one thing matters –
That wherever we go
And however we go

We hear
The music
of life .

THEODOR FONTANE

He who
desires to see
the living
God
face to face
should not
seek
HIM
in the empty
firmament of
his mind, but
in
human love.

DOSTOEVSKY

We always hope; and
in all things it is
better to hope
than to despair:
When we return to
real trust in God,
there will no
longer be room
in our soul for
fear.

GOETHE

Teach us, good Lord,
to serve Thee as Thou deservest;
to give and not to count the cost,
to fight and not
to heed the wounds,
to toil and not to seek for rest,
to labour and not
to ask for any reward,
save that of knowing
that we do Thy will.

IGNATIUS LOYOLA
✝

More or less sad are
finally all those who
are aware of things
beyond questions of
daily bread; but who
would wish to live
without this sadness,
deep and still, without
which there is no
true joy.

GOTTFRIED KELLER
✝

He who seeks God
Has already found Him.

GRAHAM GREENE

LORD JESUS CHRIST

How often was I
impatient, about to lose heart,
about to give up everything,
about to seek the
fearfully easy way
out: despair,
But you never lost
patience.
You bore a whole life
of suffering to redeem
even me.

KIERKEGAARD

Suffer
and
bear

Better days
will come.
Everything must serve
those who stand firm.
Heart, old child,

Suffer
and
bear.

CHRISTIAN MORGENSTERN

Let us have
trust in GOD
and comfort ourselves with the
thought that all is well, if it
happens according to the
Will of the Almighty,
since He knows best
what is good for our temporal
as well as eternal
happiness
and salvation.

MOZART

Our cares we can cast
on Thee, then Thou carest
for us. How can we be
troubled about the future
road, since it belongs
to Thee ? How can we
be troubled where it
leads, since it finally
but leads us to
Thee!

JOHN HENRY NEWMAN

A happy
Memory

Is on earth perhaps truer
Than happiness.

A. de MUSSET

Even in the darkest
hours of life let us
remember with comfort and
assurance that for each of
us something of paradise
is left:
in the certainty
of God's love,
which supports us,
in the beauty of
the stars and flowers
and in the happiness which
radiates from a child's eyes.

NICODEMUS

Nothing else
in the world
can make man
unhappy
but fear.
The misfortune
we suffer is
seldom if ever
as bad as that
which we fear.

SCHILLER

I believe
that when death
closes our eyes
we shall awaken
to a light, of
which our sunlight
is but the shadow.

SCHOPENHAUER

Jesus Christ

teaches men that there is
something in them which
lifts them above this life
with its hurries, its pleasures
and fears. He who understands
Christ's teaching feels like a
bird that did not know it has
wings and now suddenly realises
that it can fly, can be free
and no longer needs to fear.

TOLSTOY

How poor are they

That have not patience!

SHAKESPEARE

He who remains cheerful in spirit
and sees only the good side of
all things, who never allows
himself to be spiritually
downcast
but keeps his head high
and courage
in his heart, he sets in motion
those fine, still powers, which
make every step through life
easier for him.

RALPH WALDO TRINE

Precious little gifts of lasting value

In the same series:

Texts chosen by E. Hettinger
Translated by Dr. Peter M. Daly
Designer J. Tannheimer

Distribution:
UK: Search Press Ltd., England
USA: Kampmann & Company Inc., New York

Copyright 1986 by Leobuchhandlung, CH-St. Gallen
Modèle déposé, BIRPI
Printed in Switzerland